Original title:
Snuggle Struggle

Copyright © 2024 Creative Arts Management OÜ
All rights reserved.

Author: Arabella Whitmore
ISBN HARDBACK: 978-9916-94-208-6
ISBN PAPERBACK: 978-9916-94-209-3

Unraveled Bonds

We wrestle for the covers, oh what a sight,
One leg on my side, another in a fight.
Pillows tossed like ninja stars in the air,
Yet somehow we both end up on the bare chair.

Your cold feet sneak like ninjas in the night,
While I defend my fortress with all my might.
You laugh and snicker, it's all in good fun,
Yet I'm dizzy in this battle, where's the sun?

Comfort and Contention

In the cozy nest where feathers fly,
Your elbow jabs me, oh why, oh why?
I offer you warmth, but you take my space,
Now we're two puzzle pieces in a frantic race.

Blankets tangle like spaghetti at play,
You pull, I tug; it's the same every day.
Giggles erupt as we both go askew,
Laughter erupts, yes, that's how we do.

Cuddles of Conflict

Oh, the tender moments turn comedic quick,
As you hoard the duvet like a magic trick.
With playful jabs and soft little shoves,
This might be a war, but we say it's love.

Your snoring roars louder than a thunderstorm,
Yet I still inch closer, seeking your warmth.
With each little tussle, I can't help but grin,
This cuddly combat is where we begin.

The Push and Pull of Affection

You sip from my mug like a sneaky thief,
While I glare at you, hiding my relief.
Arm over arm, we tussle for a spot,
Who knew that cuddles could feel like a lot?

It's a game of tug-of-war every night,
I win some rounds, but you claim the light.
Yet in this chaos, our hearts stay aligned,
In the funniest struggles, true love's defined.

Bonds Tied Too Close

When blankets wrap like a tight squeeze,
And toes get tangled in a playful tease.
I try to stretch, but just can't wriggle,
Your elbow's stuck—oh, what a giggle!

We dive for covers, you steal my space,
Your pillow's my guard; it's quite the race.
Each turn is like dodging a sudden wall,
Why can't we share? Oh, this brawl's a ball!

Harmony in the Tension

In this dance of sheets, a waltz so grand,
We twirl and twist, but oh, it's quite planned.
Your feet like ice, but I'm warm as toast,
It's a nightly game; I should almost boast.

Each night's a puzzle of limbs and sighs,
With giggled protests and sleepy goodbyes.
Our little battle ignites the night,
Who knew a cuddle could yield such delight?

Cuddle Clash

Two pillows stack like a fortress tall,
But your snores declare a war, after all.
I seek the edge of this blanketed fight,
While you commandeer it—oh, what a sight!

Your arm is a weight, yet I can't complain,
In this snug melee, I feel no pain.
Each push and shove brings laughter anew,
Except when you steal my last bite of stew!

The Embrace Dilemma

Caught in a hug that's a bit too tight,
You chuckle as I squirm with all my might.
In this cozy squabble, I can't break free,
Why is your comfort so unyieldingly me?

With a wiggle and jiggle, I seek to escape,
Your playful grip is like clingy tape.
Yet through the chaos, there's warmth in our tease,
This cuddly conundrum is sure to please!

Tender Tugging

In the morning light we cling,
A battle royal, hear us sing.
Pillow forts and sheets astray,
Who can claim the bed today?

The cat jumps in to stake a claim,
Wrestling partners in a game.
Arms entangled, legs all twisted,
From dawn till dusk, we are resisted.

Each giggle adds to our delight,
Amid the chaos, what a sight!
With every push, we plant a kiss,
Stripped of anger, what a bliss.

So here we are, a tangled mess,
Laughter reigns, we must confess.
With every tug, our hearts entwine,
In this wild dance, you're still all mine.

The Commotion of Cuddles

Cuddle puddles on the floor,
Who knew warmth could start a war?
Elbows jabbing, knees collide,
Still, we laugh and choose to bide.

Soft flannel making it tough,
Wrestling blankets, it's all in love.
Joyful grumbles fill the air,
As we manage to find a chair.

With every toss, a smile beams,
A hilarious fight within our dreams.
And just as one claims victory,
The other comes back, oh woe is me!

In this playful little bout,
Tangled arms, there's no doubt.
The chaos reigns, but oh so sweet,
In every struggle, love's heartbeat.

Interwoven Intricacies

Under layers of cozy fleece,
A playful war that won't cease.
Tickles loom like unseen foes,
Braiding limbs in cunning throes.

As I pull one way, you stray,
A dizzy merry-go-round display.
Laughter bubbles, the stakes are high,
It's a cuddle fight, oh my oh my!

Every push feels like a dance,
Lost in warmth, we've lost our pants!
With every twist, we're woven tight,
In this fabric, love takes flight.

Resolute, we cannot yield,
Queens and kings upon our field.
With every grapple a new plight,
In our quilted fortress, love ignites.

Ensnared in Warmth

Wrapped in layers of woolly cheer,
A tug-of-war that draws us near.
Huddled close, we take our stand,
In this cozy, cuddly band.

Arms like vines around our frame,
Who would even dare to blame?
Knees bump, and giggles rise,
A wild party in disguise.

With every shove, the pillows zoom,
Our fortress grows and fills the room.
The more we wrangle, the more we squeal,
In this chaos, love we feel.

Heat surges through this playful brawl,
In the end, we both stand tall.
For in this warmth, two hearts unite,
Ensnared forever, and that feels right.

Battle of the Cushions

In the realm of fluffy fights,
Cushions clash with all their might.
One lands softly on my head,
While another dreams of a comfy bed.

Pillows scatter, feathers fly,
As I laugh and let out a sigh.
The couch is now a battleground,
Where laughter and fluff can both be found.

Tossing cushions, a playful spree,
As the dog joins in with glee.
My fortress made of fabric pride,
Is a tender trap, I cannot hide.

In this cozy chaos we reside,
Cushions sullen, yet we're tied.
We wrestle, tumble, roll about,
In this madcap fluff-filled bout.

Embrace Dissonance

The hug is tight, yet so perplexed,
My arms are trapped; I'm almost vexed.
One side warm, the other cold,
Is this embrace bold or just old?

The blanket's up; the sheets can't breathe,
Twisted limbs make my heart wreathe.
Laughter bubbles in tangled threads,
In this warm mess where humor spreads.

A leg is here, a foot is there,
An awkward pose beyond compare.
The night is still, the stars are bright,
Yet I'm wrestling with both hope and fright.

Here we are, in symphony,
Dissonant notes in harmony.
With every snort and giggly sigh,
We count the stars, just you and I.

Coalescing Contradictions

Caught between a dream and a scream,
With half a snore, I dare to dream.
The blanket's warm, the room is snug,
Yet I'm sprawled out like a bug.

One arm is here, the other's lost,
Like a puzzle that's been tossed.
In this twist of limbs so absurd,
I find my laughter can't be deterred.

Half awake and half asleep,
As tangled thoughts begin to creep.
A sock's on my face, how did it get there?
In the midst of oddities, I'll just declare.

Two bodies twisted, intertwined,
In this chaos, joy we find.
We wobble, giggle, laugh while we sigh,
These contradictions are our reply.

Nestled Yet Unsettled

Nestled deep in cotton's bliss,
Whispers turn to an awkward kiss.
I'm cozy, warm, and feeling fine,
But who has taken my last line?

One foot here, the other gone,
Blanket fights last till the dawn.
The cat jumps in, we start to roll,
As furry chaos takes its toll.

Sipping tea from a wayward cup,
Clumsy fingers spill it up.
We 'settle down' but not too well,
In this lively fold, how can I tell?

So snug yet restless in this space,
With laughter bright and a coffee trace.
In the midst of comfy, we thrived,
Nestled tight, we're fully alive.

Warmth in the Clutch

In the blanket fort we fight,
For the softest edge, you see.
With pillows flying, what a sight,
Claim the fluff, oh woe is me.

Your feet are cold, oh what a plight,
I'm wrapped in layers, feeling bold.
I steal the sheets, like a thief at night,
A warm embrace, but the truth be told.

Who knew a cuddle could start a war?
With laughter loud, we clash and roll.
A tug-of-war for warmth galore,
In our cozy nest, we're two halves whole.

Embrace of the Tangle

Wrapped in limbs, it's quite a mess,
You steal the cover, oh, such nerve!
I poke you back, it's pure duress,
In this dance, we find our swerve.

The cat looks on, quite entertained,
As we tumble, giggle and claw.
Your hair's a nest, oh how it's gained,
In our twisty love, there's never a flaw.

We roll and flop, like fish in sand,
A tangle of giggles and sleepy sighs.
Though tangled tight, it's all so grand,
In this playful knot, our comfort lies.

Pillow Fights of the Heart

A soft salute, and then it starts,
Feathers flying, laughter leaps.
With cunning strikes, we swap our parts,
The floor our battlefield, no time for sleep.

Dodge and weave, don't take it hard,
Each hit a giggle, slap on the cheek.
Your aim is wild, but I stand guard,
In this frolic, it's love we seek.

Down we land, in heaps so grand,
The aftermath, a chaos of fluff.
Through our laughter, hand in hand,
Pillow fights are just silly stuff.

Cozy Conflicts

The couch is claimed, my throne of fluff,
You insist on sharing, what a joke!
I give a look, it's messy enough,
But here we are, with hearts bespoke.

Your icy toes invade my space,
I shove you over, it's all in play.
With mock outrage on your face,
We giggle, roll, and laugh away.

Through playful jabs and cheeky grins,
Our little squabbles are more than fun.
In cozy conflicts, love begins,
Wrapped in warm hearts when the day is done.

Chasing Warmth

In a blanket war, we roll and twist,
Seeking the heat, we cannot resist.
Like wrestlers we tumble, giggles abound,
As socks fly off, laughter is found.

With pillows as shields, we fend off the cold,
Each grab for covers, a story unfolds.
Grappling for comfort, it's quite the event,
In this playful battle, warmth's our intent.

Emotions Undercover

Tucked in tight, a secret affair,
Under the covers, we shuffle and stare.
Faces turn red, with peals of delight,
As we navigate fluff in the dead of the night.

Whispers of laughter, snorts of surprise,
From silly defenses, where mischief lies.
Pillow fort walls, our fortress divine,
In this cozy combat, your heart beats with mine.

The Art of Holding Tight

In a twist of limbs, we find our way,
Trying to cling, as we humorously sway.
Battling for space in a blanket cocoon,
Where cuddles create a melodic tune.

The dance of our elbows, a comical fight,
As we navigate covers in the soft light.
With giggles aplenty and snickers galore,
In this tangled embrace, we always want more.

Tightly Woven

Wrapped up like burritos, snug as can be,
Your feet kick wildly, encroaching on me.
Those playful nudges, they spark such delight,
In our woven chaos, everything feels right.

As we flip and we flop, it's a merry old game,
Until someone claims the last mound of fame.
Our laughter, like sparkles, illuminates air,
In this tightly spun comfort, love shows it's flair.

Freely Frayed

Like a patchwork quilt frayed at the seams,
We tug and we pull, lost in wild dreams.
Holding on loosely, we tumble and roll,
A hilarious venture for heart and for soul.

With jests and with jabs, we stifle our cries,
As we both make a bid for the warmest prize.
Every tickle leads to an uproarious fight,
In this tangled embrace, everything feels right.

Cuddly Confrontations

In a blanket fort so snug,
Two cats debate who's the hug.
One pounces fast, then takes a chance,
While the other rolls in a goofy dance.

A tussle here, a tumble there,
Fluffy bodies everywhere!
With purrs and growls, they wrestle tight,
In fuzzy chaos, a silly sight.

The couch is now a wrestling ring,
As silly as a cat can spring.
Laughter echoes in the room,
As feathers fly in this fuzzy bloom.

When one gives up, it's not the end,
They join as one; oh, what a blend!
Two sleepy heads on a pillow rest,
In perfect peace—a cozy quest.

Heartfelt Hurdles

A race to the sofa, who will win?
Tails wagging wild, let the fun begin!
One leaps high, the other dives low,
In a cuddly chase, they steal the show.

Pillow forts and hidden nooks,
In quest for warmth, they grabbed the books.
Yet in this plushy, tangled mess,
A battle brews, oh what a stress!

The coffee mug now holds the prize,
A human's lap, the purrfect size.
But playful paws plead for the spot,
A tug-of-war, who gets the lot?

A final leap, a furry flop,
All cuddles end in a playful drop.
With laughter shared and sleepy sighs,
They find their peace in sleepy ties.

Haven or Hustle

In the morning light, they plot and scheme,
A cozy pile or an epic dream?
One's in charge of the fluff and fold,
While the other finds mischief, brave and bold.

Socks are scattered, and bedsheets tossed,
Their playful antics can't be lost.
A race for space, who takes the prize?
A wriggly tangle full of surprise!

A summit of cushions becomes their peak,
Each little nuzzle hides a squeak.
With cheeky grins and sneaky paws,
They tumble down without a pause.

At last a truce, they make amends,
Clinging tight, their laughter blends.
In soft embrace, they find their bliss—
With every tussle, it's love they kiss.

The Hug Paradox

In a world where hugs can bind,
Two pals collide, oh what a find!
One's too big, the other just right,
In a twist of fate, it's a comical sight.

A bear hug here, a gentle squeeze,
One gets wiggly, the other just flees.
As they chase each other round the room,
Giggles erupt, dispelling the gloom.

Through flailing limbs and playful shoves,
Each tries to claim a share of loves.
But tangled together, they start to roll,
A belly laugh is the ultimate goal!

Pinned on the floor, wrapped up tight,
They find the joy in their little fight.
With hearts aflutter and smiles wide,
In this playful mess, love cannot hide.

Nesting Challenges

In a pile of pillows, we start to fight,
Rolling and tumbling, oh what a sight!
You take my blanket, I grab your sock,
A cozy battleground, time to unlock.

Laughter erupts as I steal your space,
A woven maze, it's quite the race!
We wrestle for room on our fluffy throne,
In our fortress of cushions, we're never alone.

Every shift creates a raucous cheer,
With giggles and grumbles that only we hear.
The art of the cuddle, a tactical sport,
Mastering the chaos, our favorite resort.

The Dilemma of Affection

You want a hug, but I need my space,
A tangled embrace turns into a chase.
I shuffle away, you pull me back tight,
Wrapped in your arms, it gives me a fright!

Your cheek on my shoulder, it's snug as a bug,
But my arm's gone numb in this innermost hug.
Should I wiggle free or snuggle right in?
This love-twist tango has turned into a spin.

Every sigh's a comedy, a playful tease,
Bound in affection, we both aim to please.
Yet the push and the pull make quite the show,
In this love-filled tug-of-war, time seems to flow.

Blanket Brawls

Underneath the covers, a battle unfolds,
Layer by layer, the warmth we hold.
I tug and I pull, you cling with a grin,
In our cozy arena, let the games begin!

The sheets are our canvas, a wrestle divine,
Rolling and jostling, it's your turn, it's mine!
A fortress of fabric, a quilt of delight,
We fight for the center, hoot with delight.

One leg draped over, my foot in your face,
You laugh as I crawl to reclaim my place.
In fluff and in giggles, we navigate tight,
Making memories with our blanket delight.

Clasping Conflicts

Your hand in mine, it's a slippery grip,
Trying to blend, but we often trip.
A warm little knot that's tangled and tight,
Lost in the wrestle of day and of night.

Trying to hold on while you slip away,
Your wild acrobatics lead me astray.
I grasp at your sleeve, you laugh and you swirl,
In this playful tussle, we twirl and we whirl.

The clasp of our fingers wraps in a dance,
Twisting and turning, indulging in chance.
A short-lived struggle that brings us to cheer,
With each little conflict, together we steer.

War of the Warmth

In winter's grasp we hide away,
Beneath the blankets where we play.
One foot out, a quick retreat,
To claim the warmth, a daring feat.

A tussle over covers wide,
My side, your side, where to abide?
Elbows jostle, laughter erupts,
My cozy fortress—totally MUCKED!

Curling like cats in a sunbeam,
Who would've thought this is the theme?
Furry socks and slippers dash,
In this duel, who'll have the last laugh?

Defeated yet giggling, we yield,
One blanket, one heart—together we shield.
Though battles ensue with tickles and glee,
In the war of the warmth, you're winning with me!

Rugged Relations

Two pillows clash like knights in quest,
A cozy battle with no time to rest.
Cups of tea on the bedside stand,
While soft throws limit our command.

Who claims the edge of the bed tonight?
With feet that sneak like a thief in flight.
Hands that pull, and then they withdraw,
In this rough-and-tumble draw of law.

Crafty moves and silly ruses,
Each attempt could lead to bruises.
Pillow fort walls tumble and fall,
Yet laughter's the victor in this brawl.

Once more we clash for the perfect space,
But every tussle leads to your face.
And as the night falls, we cap the fun,
Wrap up in warmth; we both have won!

The Clutch Conundrum

Morning light creeps, up we rise,
But holds no bounds for cozy ties.
A game of tug and a cheeky grin,
Clutching the sheets, where do we begin?

Twists and turns in our sleepy land,
One brave move, oh, wasn't it grand?
A blanket rolled as we fight the chill,
I steal it back; you come in for the thrill.

Grapples ensue on plush pillows soft,
In pursuit of boudoir, we laugh and scoff.
And though we wedged in the warmest night,
The more I clutch, the more we fight!

A truce is made when yawns break free,
With one last tug, you snuggle close to me.
Though struggles abound in our cozy nest,
In the clutch of love, I'm truly blessed!

Affectionate Fray

Shivering thoughts of winter's call,
Blankets piled up like a warm wall.
Underneath layers, the heat is on,
In this playful brawl, we've both drawn.

With coffee cups like shields in hand,
We laugh as we plot our small war plan.
A diving leap for the last warm spot,
Yet you trip me, oh, you sly tot!

Scuffles and giggles ignite the night,
Gathered like squirrels in a frenzied flight.
Laughter erupts in the tussles we make,
As we fight for warmth, our hearts awake.

The cutest skirmish in the realm of snug,
With every poke and playful hug.
And when it's all done, we smile and lay,
In this affectionate fray, we find our way!

Warmth vs. Solitude

In a blanket wrap, I feel delight,
But there's a fight for space each night.
One side hogs it, the other protests,
Jostling limbs make it hard to rest.

Warm and cozy, we both decree,
Yet limbs entangle like chains of glee.
Laughter erupts as we squish and shove,
Comfort blends in this tussle of love.

A sneaky elbow finds my waist,
Tickles bring giggles, oh such a taste!
But oh! That foot which drapes on my head,
In this warm battle, I laugh instead.

So here we are, entwined as we dream,
In our cuddly chaos, we make quite a team.
With every tug and pull of the night,
Our funny fight brings such pure delight.

Intertwined Irritations

Together we lie, seeking delight,
But your snoring is quite the fright!
I nudge and push, can you please hush?
Yet somehow I quickly lose my rush.

Pillow wars break out, oh what a sight,
Each swing and miss makes our laughter ignite.
Fun and fray dance in the sheets,
While tangled sheets wrap up our feats.

Your cold toes sneak in, causing distress,
While I roll away in a blanket mess.
Yet here we are, with giggles and sighs,
In every mishap, joy surely lies.

Navigating chaos in the dark,
Our cuddly wrestling leaves quite a mark.
No retreat, no surrender, through night's embrace,
We find our humor in this tangled space.

Secured Yet Strained

Tucked in tight, we share the quilt,
But who knew love could feel like guilt?
Jostling for warmth, a playful plight,
In a cozy embrace, we ignite the night.

Squeezed so close, a couple of clowns,
Your knee on my side makes me frown.
Yet laughter slips through, oh what a twist,
In this complicated warmth, I can't resist.

Air gets tight with each tiny shove,
But your big hugs are what I love.
Just when we think we've found our way,
I steal your blanket, but you start to sway.

A wrestling match tucked in our lair,
In a pillow fight, who'll win fair?
Yet as I tumble, and you start to pout,
We find our joy, that's what it's about.

The Complicated Comfort

Laughter erupts in a cuddly heap,
But with every snuggle, I lose my sleep.
Your mismatched socks find room on my face,
In this entangled, warm, playful space.

With pillows as shields, we wage our war,
I'll guard my side, and you'll guard your floor.
Each poke and jab brings giggles galore,
In this cozy chaos, I couldn't ask for more.

With tangled limbs, the night spins on,
In the struggle for space, we've both grown fond.
What once was a quarrel for room in our bed,
Is now a dance of warmth instead.

Though we wriggle and scramble, it's quite the delight,
In this funny melee, our hearts feel light.
So bring on the chaos, I say with a grin,
For every tussle tells us love's within.

Cozy Conflicts

When blankets battle for the bed,
I fight with pillows, bump my head.
The cat will steal my cozy space,
Yet still I hold a warm embrace.

A quilt that's just too small, you see,
Wraps me tighter than a burrito, whee!
With limbs entangled, I can't quite move,
The thermostat's my next big groove.

In winter, socks are lost in pairs,
And beneath the sheets, there are snares.
I roll and tumble, there's much at stake,
This wriggly dance, for fun's own sake!

A cup of tea spills, I jump with glee,
As we rewrite the rules to be.
With laughter spilling from the seams,
We find our way back to shared dreams.

The Tight Squeeze Dilemma

Two cats, one lap, it's quite the test,
Who will claim the spot that's best?
One paw goes high, another's low,
I'm stuck like jam in a tight, warm row.

Warmth wraps around, yet I can't breathe,
Legs are intertwined, I hardly seethe.
A snicker rises, a playful plight,
As we shift and shake into the night.

Oh, the couch becomes a wrestling ring,
A love-hate match that makes hearts sing.
Those furry thugs, they declare their claim,
But I just laugh; it's all a game.

With every tussle, a giggle flows,
In cozy corners, my spirit grows.
We may be trapped in this cuddle fight,
But oh what joy in soft twilight!

Serenity or Strain

In a hammock meant for two, so wide,
I inch and twitch, you slip and slide.
This gentle sway, a calming ride,
Yet causes chaos, and I'm denied.

A squeeze too tight, I hear you sigh,
Can't pass the snacks, oh how I try.
You munch too loud, I hide my grin,
As we tumble into the snack bin.

Fuzzy socks, they dance around,
Legs like pretzels on the ground.
A chill gets in, we start to fight,
Over the blanket that's just too slight.

And yet through all the playful strife,
What a glorious, funny life!
In cozy mess, our hearts entwine,
Every giggle, a sign we shine.

Embrace Enigma

Holding tight in our crazy nest,
With limbs all twisted, we jest the best.
A knot of limbs, a jumbled tune,
We laugh it off beneath the moon.

My elbow jabs your side, oh dear,
But giggles drown out all the fear.
A fortress made from fluff and cheer,
Unlocks the secrets we hold so near.

In this warm chaos, love finds a way,
Through every nudge, we bravely play.
You steal the sheets, I shriek and shout,
Yet that's what life's all about.

So here's to tight spots that we embrace,
In this puzzling dance, we'll find our place.
With laughter ringing, we rise and fall,
Two hearts forever, that's the call.

Cozy Quandaries

In the blanket fort we share,
Tangled limbs and playful stares.
Should I scoot or stay in place?
Wriggling leads to quite the chase.

Your toe creeps into my side,
While I giggle and try to hide.
Who will claim the puffiest spot?
This cozy tug-of-war is hot!

Clothes are strewn and pillows flew,
As we both play the 'who's in who?'
The cat stares down with judging eyes,
As laughter in the chaos flies.

A sneeze goes off, and we both shake,
What a mess from our little quake.
Yet here we are, snug as can be,
In this silly warm cacophony!

Strains Beneath Soft Covers

Pillow fights with no real aim,
As we laugh while we stake our claim.
You take my warmth, I steal your space,
Who knew this would become a race?

Legs tangled up, a knot so tight,
While we squabble through the night.
If only there were room to breathe,
But this amateur wrestling won't leave.

You stretch too far, I block the flow,
A cozy jail, don't you know?
Your hand is warm, but so is mine,
In this card game of 'who's divine?'

The clock ticks on, our dreams entwined,
As the world outside continues blind.
Two silly souls, a pillow heap,
In this blanket war, we laugh and leap!

The Dance of Closeness

In our waltz of twisted sheets,
Two left feet meet mischief's beats.
Your laugh, a tumble, I can't resist,
This floor's a mess—we're on the list.

Around the room, we spin and twirl,
With mismatched socks, we laugh and whirl.
Your elbow nudges—oops, my bad!
This move's the best I ever had!

As the night deepens, hugs grow tight,
While shadows play beneath the light.
Who knew a dance could raise a fuss?
Yet in this chaos, there's still us.

With every stumble, we both declare,
That nothing quite matches this rare affair.
Two clumsy hearts in a timing fray,
In this awkward dance, we forever stay!

Complexity of the Caress

Your hand slips underneath my chin,
Is that a poke, or sweet begin?
Soft tussles turn into a fight,
What began as cute, climbed to new heights.

With every touch, we laugh and tease,
Navigating this puzzle with ease.
The softest whispers, a playful shove,
In this cozy mess, it's all about love.

Do I tickle, or do I pout?
In our tangled sheets, there's never doubt.
Yet with each squish, our mess unfolds,
Tales of warmth that never grow old.

Caught between laughter and a sigh,
Cuddly conundrums, oh my, oh my!
In a world where chaos gets a goal,
Our complexity shines with warmth in our soul.

The Clutch of Comfort

In blankets piled high, we wrestle with glee,
A dog with the hiccups, as loud as can be.
Your foot's in my face, my elbow's in yours,
Together we tumble, love's chaotic chores.

The popcorn is flying, oh what a fight,
You nibble my chips, but that's just alright.
Together we laugh, despite the tight squeeze,
This awkward entanglement brings me such ease.

Harmony or Hustle?

Your arm drapes like a blanket, heavy and warm,
While I sidestep your snoring, a quirky alarm.
Wrapped up in a conundrum, a comfy pig pile,
Who needs a personal space? Not us, that's our style!

The remote's lost again, buried under the fluff,
We blame it on each other, but we're both just too tough.
We bicker and giggle, it's all in good fun,
In this cozy mayhem, we've truly both won.

The Push and Pull of Affection

You tug at the covers, I cling on for dear life,
A tug-of-war battle, my partner in strife.
With each gentle nudge, I'm laughing inside,
Who knew that sweet cuddles could come with such pride?

Your leg's on my side, I wrinkle my nose,
As you steal all the sheets, my frustration just grows.
Yet somehow I cherish this chaotic embrace,
In this playful skirmish, we've found our best place.

Warmth's Tugging Truths

In the frosty night air, we battle to stay,
A duvet disaster, our own little fray.
Your feet are like ice, yet you've taken the space,
With laughter and elbow nudges, we find our own grace.

Then comes the tickle fight, a soft playful clash,
As warmth and affection create quite the splash.
Amidst every tussle, I see love's true art,
In this comical chaos, you've captured my heart.

Tender Tangles

In the morning, I reach for you,
A pillow fort, our cozy view.
But you twist and turn like a wily cat,
My sheets are now a knotty splat!

Your legs entwined like spaghetti strands,
In bed we form our tangled brands.
I laugh at how we fight for space,
A wrestling match in our soft embrace!

Cuddles sweet as cookie dough,
Yet limbs revolt, and off they go.
You steal the blanket, I chase your feet,
Somehow, it turns into a comic feat!

So here we lie, a mess of dreams,
Our laughter echoes, or so it seems.
In love's absurdity, we find a thrill,
With every tangle, we love you still!

Hugging Hardships

When you hug me, it's a joyful task,
But not too tight—I cannot gasp!
Your arms like vines, they wrap me tight,
In this funny battle, who's wrong, who's right?

I try to wriggle, escape the squeeze,
You hold me on like I'm a cheese!
With every pinch, I cannot quite tell,
If this is heaven or a cozy hell.

Shared blankets turning into a fight,
You pull me close, oh what a sight!
As laughter breaks through each little shrug,
Turned upside down, it's a hugging bug!

So let's hold tight and giggle some more,
With every struggle, I love you to the core.
In our cuddly chaos, we find our way,
Two misfits thriving every day!

The Great Hug Conflict

Once upon a time in our cozy lair,
We faced a clash, a hug-filled scare.
Our arms entwined like a knotted vine,
Who's winning here? You or me, divine?

When I lean in, you lean out,
Oh the tussle, oh the pout!
Two hearts battling for the best part,
Every hug feels like a work of art!

I declare, a truce is due,
But then you tackle, it's true, it's true!
With every shiver and every smile,
Our playful war is worth the while.

So meet me in this hug parade,
As laughter fuels our love crusade.
With every struggle, we light up the night,
In our hug conflict, everything feels right!

Affection's Anxieties

In our cozy nook, there's a little dread,
When trying to cuddle, you turn your head.
I want to squeeze, you want to glide,
In this snuggle dance, we can't decide!

Your giggles rise when I pin you down,
Yet you plot your escape like a royal crown.
I chase you back with a playful tickle,
One moment it's cuteness, then chaos is fickle!

Every hug converts to a wild game,
With flailing limbs and a laugh so tame.
We battle for space on this love-soaked shore,
In every anxious hug, I love you more!

So let's embrace our cuddly fate,
Where every struggle feels first-rate.
In the quirks of love, let's find our beat,
In affection's charm, we'll always compete!

Wrapped Up in Chaos

In a blanket fight we dive,
Tangled limbs, we barely thrive,
Coffee spills, a splashy spree,
Laughter echoes, wild and free.

Couch cushions fly like birds,
Amidst the giggles, silly words,
A puppy joins, with joyful barks,
Chaos reigns, oh, what a lark!

The popcorn flies across the room,
As we wrestle in our cozy doom,
One falls off without a clue,
How did I end up stuck with you?

Pajamas on, we roll and spin,
Who would win? Let the games begin!
Amid the mess, my heart does cheer,
In every giggle, you're my dear.

Tension in the Tenderness

Cuddle time, but not quite right,
Elbows jabbing, snug and tight,
You steal the covers, what a move,
My sleepy self starts to groove.

Whispers float in comfy snare,
Somehow we're both pulling hair,
Pillow forts with all our might,
As midnight laughter takes to flight.

A game of tug, oh what a sight,
Two blankets wrapped in silly fights,
Between the cuddles there's a flair,
For every twist, I'll still be there.

But then we stop, our laughter streams,
In the struggle, love redeems,
With every nudge, we make it right,
In just a mess, feels so light.

Twists of Togetherness

You grab the remote, I claim the space,
Our sides collide in a cosmic race,
A tumble here, a giggle there,
Together wrapped in joyful care.

Feet entangled, a dance on the floor,
The couch, our ship, oh, to explore,
Adventure's written in midnight snacks,
Between the bickering, love attacks.

A race to snatch the last cool treat,
Laughter erupts, can't feel defeat,
With each twist and silly slip,
Our fun expands, don't let it trip!

Between the pillows, chaos dwells,
Stories whisper where laughter swells,
In every twist, a bond shines bright,
Together tangled, fierce delight.

When Comfort Grips Too Tight

In our fortress of fluffy pillows,
Spaces shrink like tiny swallows,
Cuddles morph to tangle knots,
Tickle wars become our spots.

The popcorn's gone, just crumbs remain,
A sticky mishap on the pane,
We lurch and sway in cozy strife,
Navigating humor in this life.

When arms embrace, and hugs are free,
Yet here you are, right on my knee,
Can't wiggle out of this warm nest,
But with this chaos, I feel blessed.

With snickers shared under blanket skies,
In every nudge, a love that flies,
Through struggles soft, we find our song,
In this mix, is where we belong.

The Dilemma of Desire

In a blanket fort, we clash,
Your side's too warm, I'll make a dash.
Popcorn flies in wild retreat,
As I defend my comfy seat.

Pillow fights turn into wars,
Tossing cushions like a chore.
Who knew cuddling could ignite,
A playful brawl in the moonlight?

We reach for snacks, arms intertwine,
Your gummy bear versus my twine.
Tangled limbs in a giggle spree,
How did this mess become so spree?

Yet when we're lost in plush embrace,
I wonder if I'll lose my place.
But laughter echoes, love's the snare,
In this delightful, cozy lair.

Fretful Fondness

Socks collide beneath the sheets,
A tug-of-war with hidden feats.
My coffee's gone, it's now your brew,
But your slippers look quite askew.

Tiny toes invade my space,
Elbow jabs—oh what a race!
Just when I think I've made my mark,
You steal the sheets, it's cold and dark!

A nibble here, a wink from there,
The popcorn fluffs fly through the air.
In this couch maze, we spin and flop,
How many snacks before we stop?

With every bump and little fight,
We find our way, hearts feeling light.
In this chaos, love takes flight,
Each struggle's worth the laughter's height.

Close Quarters Quandary

Here we are in tight confines,
Your elbow's mine—how can that shine?
Strawberries shared, but napkins fail,
What's worse? The crumbs or the trail?

Wrestling pillows in late-night chats,
I claim the space, you argue that.
But when you smile, it's hard to plot,
These friendly fights are quite the lot!

Chips are crunched amidst the fray,
As we concoct our silly play.
Your laughter bounces, mine takes flight,
In this bumpy cuddle delight.

Tangled limbs on this blissful ride,
Though battling for the golden side.
Love's the prize when the night is done,
Two hearts tangled, oh what fun!

Tiramisu Tangle

Dessert for two, let's take a bite,
But your fork steals mine in the night.
Layers stacked like our wild dreams,
Each spoonful punctured by giggle screams.

Creamy layers, a sweet ballet,
Your hands are slick; that's not okay!
With every bite, there's a small fight,
As tiramisu takes to the flight.

Fingers sticky, laughter burst,
Who knew dessert could turn to first?
With every nibble, sweetened bliss,
We grab a bite and sneak a kiss.

In this cake mess, we find our grace,
A tangle of joy in a scrumptious space.
So here's to fights over dessert divine,
With you close, it's perfectly fine!

Fondness Fracas

When blankets tangle, we start to fight,
You steal the covers, oh what a sight!
I wiggle and squirm, your grip won't break,
Together we wrestle, for warmth's sweet sake.

With pillows as shields, we clash like pros,
A giggle erupts, as the chaos grows.
Who will stay warm in this feathery war?
Come morning, we're friends, and we cuddle once more.

You pinch my side, I poke your nose,
Laughter erupts as the tension grows.
Our cozy combat, a dance so absurd,
We fight just for fun, it's all quite preferred.

As dawn grows bright, our battle is through,
A truce made with coffee, just me and you.
In sheets entangled, we finally rest,
This fondness affair is the very best.

The Comfort Competition

In a hammock so cozy, we both aim to sit,
But who gets more room? This is it!
Elbows and knees, in a clumsy ballet,
We teeter and rock, in our game of delay.

Cuddles turn tactical, oh it's quite grand,
With snacks in the middle, it's all gotten planned.
You want the chips, but I crave the dip,
In this comfort contest, we never let rip.

Our laughter erupts with each little poke,
Under a blanket, it's hardly a cloak.
You snatch at my leg, while I grab your socks,
A playful skirmish, avoiding the clocks.

As the evening sets, and our game fizzles out,
We snicker and giggle, no worries or doubt.
Our comfort competition ends with a grin,
As we cozy up tight, let the fun begin!

Love's Lingering Tension

As night creeps in, two sides of the bed,
You steal the space and rest your head.
I shove a pillow, reclaiming my zone,
Yet your foot finds mine, and we chuckle alone.

There's a battle of warmth beneath the sheets,
A dance of the limbs, my heart gently beats.
We laugh through the tussle, the night-time chase,
In this lighthearted fray, we find our place.

You snore like a bear, I giggle with glee,
Your blanket fortress is a sight to see.
Yet when you reach out, I can't help but sigh,
In love's lingering tension, our hearts fly high.

From tussles to tickles, the nights wearing on,
We settle the score, till the break of dawn.
In this playful fight, every giggle, a win,
With you by my side, let the fun begin!

Affectionate Aversities

When we clash for space, it turns into fun,
Rolling and rumbling, under the sun.
I swipe the last cookie, you holler with glee,
In your mock outrage, I can't help but agree.

Your elbow grazes, as I try to lay flat,
We tussle for more, then settle like that.
We dance with the blankets, a twirl here and there,
In affectionate aversities, love fills the air.

Each jab and each poke, they're tenderly meant,
In the bubble of laughter, our time's well spent.
Your snickers echo, as I let out a sigh,
In this playful brawl, we're over the sky.

With each little fight, we grow even closer,
It's a paradox, our love, like a rollercoaster.
So here's to the scrimmages, the playful dismay,
In affectionate aversities, we'll always stay!

Clashing Comforts

Two blankets battle for my heart,
One's a cloud, the other's a dart.
In cozy realms they fiercely vie,
While I just want to watch and sigh.

Socks mismatched, I can't decide,
One's too big, the other's tried.
A fuzzy friend upon my lap,
But it's a dance, not a nap.

Pillows piled like a mountain high,
But one slips out, oh me, oh my!
Cushions land in awkward heaps,
While laughter in the chaos creeps.

I wrestle with my duvet tight,
A superhero in the night.
A twist, a turn, a tumble and roll,
Yet still I reach for my bedtime goal.

Heated Hugs

Arms entwined in a feathery clash,
Too warm to breathe, oh what a smash!
Like two bears in a frantic embrace,
I can't escape this cozy race.

Sweaters bunch, oh what a sight,
I'm freezing, but they're burning bright.
We giggle through the tangled fight,
As we dance in a fabric plight.

A cat joins in with furry grace,
Insisting on its rightful space.
With claws that pinch and purrs that tease,
We question, can we really seize?

Tangled limbs in a wild display,
More laugh than sleep, we drift away.
The warmth of chaos feels so right,
As we surrender to the night.

Softness and Unease

A plushy fortress, soft yet tough,
But one wrong bounce, and it's too rough!
The cushions giggle, the blankets squirm,
As comfort battles with a squishy term.

With feathery foes that poke and tease,
Do I want calm, or playful ease?
A tug-of-war with sheets and throws,
When will my bedtime bliss bestow?

In every twist, an echoing sigh,
Do I laugh or do I cry?
The realms of comfort, a tangled thread,
But who knew chaos could spread?

A burrito wrap with limbs that strain,
While a ticklish breeze brings on the rain.
I giggle through this quilted fight,
As I finally bid the day goodnight.

Intimacy in Friction

A blanket tug-of-war begins,
Tossing pillows, battling grins.
In the fray, we waltz and sway,
Creating chaos on display.

With every stretch, a little cringe,
Who could know a wrinkle's binge?
Our cuddle fest becomes a maze,
As laughter turns into a craze.

Legs entwined like vines gone mad,
It's funny how it turns so bad.
Ticklish jabs and playful yells,
The clashing feels like soft love spells.

In these moments, sweet absurd,
With stolen kisses and beyond words.
With every fumble, a spark awaits,
Warmed by the fun that love creates.

Squeeze Tensions

In a blanket pile, we wage the war,
Twisted limbs, can't reach the door.
Your foot's on my hair, my elbow's in sight,
Deciding who moves brings faux fright.

Giggles turn to grumbles, a playful scene,
Trying to fit on the couch—no room to glean.
A pillow fort shields, yet there's no escape,
Who knew cuddling could shape such a landscape?

As you steal the covers, a smirk on your face,
I retaliate quickly, reclaiming my space.
We laugh and we tussle, it's love's little game,
That cozy dilemma, it's never the same.

But in all this chaos, one truth shines bright,
We'll squish and we'll fumble till morning light.
Through each little struggle, our bond grows more,
In this cozy feud, we continually soar.

Cozy Clutch

Caught in a crook, you're a master thief,
Snatching my side with no sign of grief.
Your knees like a vise, my quilt a tight wrap,
Where comfort ends, and I ponder the nap.

Every twist and turn, a strategic plight,
How can it be wrong when it feels so right?
Yet each poke and prodding brings giggles galore,
In this silly dance, we both ask for more.

A tug at my arm, a laugh in the air,
Your sleepy grin says we make quite the pair.
Though pillows clash loudly and blankets do fly,
It's perfectly crazy, oh my, oh my!

Wrapped in this hold, we wrestle and tease,
Nothing's more fun than a cozy unease.
With every bumpy cuddle, a chuckle resounds,
In this joyful tussle, true love's what's found.

Lullaby of Discontent

At night, we're two peas in a bumpy pod,
Your snoring a symphony, a melody odd.
Each kick and each shove is a song to my ear,
A lullaby born from love, laced with sheer cheer.

You claim that warm spot like a dog on a bone,
As if this whole bed is somehow your throne.
I nestle and wiggle, no peace to be found,
Yet laughter erupts from this chaos around.

I mutter sweet nothings with a comical flair,
About how I'm squished like a bear in a lair.
But in the uproar, a truth starts to glow,
Such discord's a treasure we gladly bestow.

So serenade me, dear, with your jumbled charms,
We'll laugh through the night, safe in each other's arms.
In a raucous embrace, we fiend for a chance,
To tango in slumber, this wild little dance.

The Conflicted Caress

Your elbow's a weapon, a jab from the west,
While your foot finds my side, oh, what a jest!
Caught in this tangle, a comedy unfolds,
In the cozy embrace, our true love upholds.

You giggle and wiggle, your antics a sight,
Like a starfish claiming the bed every night.
Each time I roll over, it's a tactical game,
Determined to snuggle, and yet who's to blame?

With laughter and grumbles, we push and we pull,
This clumsy ballet makes my heart feel full.
Should I grab my pillow, or should I just stay?
In this funny pursuit, is it love or a fray?

Yet every dispute turns to fun in the end,
Your chaotic affection, my favorite trend.
In the tangled sheets lies our love's sweet embrace,
Through all the tensions, we've found our own space.

The Battle of Blankets

In a pile so grand, we both dive in,
But my dear, this feels like a tug-of-war win.
Your side is warmer, oh how I plead,
Yet you steal the cover, oh yes, indeed.

I pull and I tug, it's quite the show,
You grin like a cat, while I'm sunk below.
The comforter's fortress, it's stitched with glee,
But I won't give up—come cuddle with me!

With each twist and turn, I battle the quilt,
This war over warmth, oh what have I built?
Laughter erupts as we wrestle in fun,
In the end, we both know, it's love that we've won.

As blankets get twisted, the laughter is bright,
Who knew a soft sheet could spark such a fight?
With every warm squabble, we both take a stand,
In the battle of blankets, we win hand in hand.

Love's Entangled Threads

Together we weave this crazy thread,
Each knot ties us closer, that's what you said.
But my scarf is tangled; it's a sight for sore eyes,
How did this mess happen? Oh me, oh my!

You chuckle and tease as you pull on my yarn,
We trip over fibers, it's quite the alarm.
I swear it was neat, but now it's a case,
Of love turning garments into a race.

In crochet disasters, we find the delight,
Your hands full of knots, a comical sight.
We giggle and twist, dispelling the gloom,
As our fingers get tangled, we burst into bloom.

When socks become monsters, and scarves turn to snakes,

We'll laugh through our stitches with all of these flakes.
In a tangle of love, we find joy and cheer,
Each twist is a treasure, my dear, you're so near.

Fortress of Affection

Cushions piled high, they reach for the sky,
Your fortress of comfort, I can't pass by.
I scale the soft pillows with hope in my heart,
But you guard the entrance, oh clever and smart.

With laughter I climb, it's a valiant quest,
Only to find you've made it the best.
A moat made of laughter encircles the space,
While I'm left to wonder, where's my resting place?

Each cushion a challenge as I try to get in,
You giggle and tease, "You'll never win!"
But I keep on climbing in this playful fray,
To share in your fortress, come watch me, I sway.

In the end, we collapse in a heap of delight,
Your fortress of love is a comical sight.
With laughter and warmth, we both take a seat,
In this castle of cushions, our hearts feel complete.

Tension in the Twine

A ball of twine rolls, oh what a surprise,
You tug on your end, I can see it in your eyes.
With each gentle pull, the tension does rise,
This playful tug-of-war is filled with smiles and sighs.

You giggle out loud as you start to entwine,
Your hands dance about with that mischievous line.
Each knot is a joy, each loop brings a laugh,
In the game of love, we forgot the rough path.

A lasso of giggles, we're caught in the bind,
As knots interweave like a poem, unlined.
With every new twirl, our laughter ignites,
In a battle of yarn, we create little flights.

As threads come together, we craft such a mix,
Our hearts are the fabric, oh what a complex.
In the twine of our joy, we're forever aligned,
With each playful tug, our love weaves entwined.

Huddle Havoc

In a corner we bounce, a fluffy parade,
Paws in a twist, our plans have all strayed.
Nap time turns comical, a snort and a sneeze,
While tangled like yarn, we fight for some ease.

The blanket a mountain, we're lost in its fold,
Wiggling and giggling, both daring and bold.
A tumble, a shuffle, into laughter we dive,
In chaos we thrive, oh how we survive!

Cookies on a table, oh what a delight,
But reach, and you stretch, and it turns into a fight.
A whiff of the sugar, a paw for a snack,
Who knew that our love could lead to a snack attack?

With pillows as shields, and laughter the key,
In our little debacle, there's no need to flee.
As partners in chaos, we've made quite a mess,
But the joy in our huddle? It's nothing but bless!

The Quandary of Closeness

Fluffy layers stacked, like a heap of wool,
Here comes the dilemma, oh isn't it cruel!
We cuddle and giggle, yet fight for some space,
Why is this comfort a furry arms race?

Squeezed in the corner, I poke and I prod,
With warmth and confusion, my mind feels quite flawed.
Too cozy together, yet bumps start to show,
This joy brings a puzzle, like a dog in a bow.

A game of contention, who wins with their flair?
With barks and with meows, it's hard to declare!
Round and round we tumble, each seeking a spot,
Both loving and loathing this jumbled up plot.

Yet laughter erupts, we can't quite resist,
In this comedic mess, how could we be missed?
The quandary of closeness not easily tamed,
But we wouldn't trade this, even if it's unnamed!

Embrace Entropy

Underneath a blanket, a furry explosion,
The couch is a ship on a sea of commotion.
With tails as the sails, we navigate woe,
How is it, in chaos, such harmony grows?

A wild tumble here, and a squeal over there,
As each little mischief brings giggles to share.
A game of intent, or perhaps it's a race,
In the midst of this cuddly chaotic embrace.

Rising up for a snack, we're tripping and falling,
In every small clash, we're both loudly calling.
Yet somehow it's grand, this mess we create,
A track of our joy, in each tumble and fate.

So here we entangle, in warmth and delight,
In our funny adventure, everything feels right.
With pillows as shields, we embrace pure galore,
Comedic chaos, who could ask for more?

Hearthside Hostility

In the hearth's warm glow, we're packed like sardines,
Fur flying like confetti, oh how cute you seem!
But wait, what's this tussle? The battle ensues,
For the biggest patch of warmth—who's got the best views?

A paw in my face, and a tail in my ear,
While I wrestle for comfort, I fight through the cheer.
The sofa, it shudders, we bounce with a jolt,
Yet laughter erupts with each crazy cat bolt.

Shared snuggles ignite little sparks of delight,
But take one wrong step, and it turns into a fight.
A theft of the blanket, it's all out mayhem,
As snoring turns vocal, in the midst of this gem.

Yet through all the madness, our bond only grows,
In our hearthside tirades, true comedy flows.
With a wink and a nudge, we find our own way,
Together in chaos, we laugh through the day!

Sweet Discomfort

In the cozy nook we try to fit,
Each limb a puzzle piece, a bit.
You steal the blanket, my toes grow cold,
Yet somehow, it's a sight to behold.

Your elbow jabs me like a playful poke,
I laugh aloud, it's a comical joke.
One arm pinned down, I can't turn away,
This tangled dance? Another day!

Laughter bubbles as we wrestle tight,
Like kittens at play, oh what a sight!
With every shift, a newfound grin,
In this sweet chaos, love's sure to win.

So here we are, a mismatched pair,
Entwined in joy without a care.
Though comfort's fleeting, let's celebrate,
This funny mess that we create.

A Chaotic Caress

Two bodies merge, a blanket fight,
You squeeze too tight, I gasp in fright.
We tumble over pillows galore,
What was cozy has turned into war!

Your knee finds my side, oh what a thrill,
I wriggle and giggle, can't keep still.
With every nudge and playful shove,
This crazy chaos, oh how I love!

The thermostat rises, the covers retreat,
A dance of limbs, silly and sweet.
Amidst all the tussles, the laughter rings,
Wrapped in this mess, joy surely clings.

In this tangled web of limbs and sheets,
Every battle's a victory, every clash repeats.
So let's embrace this fun little mess,
Together forever, in cuddly distress!

Quarrel in the Quilt

Underneath the quilt, a bumpy road,
You hog the warmth, a heaviness bestowed.
With grumpy faces, we pull and we tug,
My side is bare, oh what a shrug!

Your dreams invade my peaceful nights,
You snore like thunder, oh what a fright!
I shove and poke, a playful attack,
In this quilted battle, there's no turning back.

The laughter erupts, we fumble and twist,
Another pillow launched, oh what a miss!
Our sleepy skirmish, a fuzzy embrace,
In this quilted chaos, we find our place.

Though each tussle may wake the dawn,
In this quilt of love, we'll always carry on.
With every struggle woven tight,
In our funny battle, everything's right.

Heartfelt Resistance

With one last gasp, I close my eyes,
Your wandering hands, oh my, what a surprise!
A gentle tug leads to a wild chase,
In this tender fight for warmth and space.

You claim the sheets like a prized possession,
While I plot my crafty interception.
The wrestle is soft, yet the victory sweet,
In heartfelt resistance, we find our beat.

With every nudge, there's a teasing grin,
Caught in this tangle, where do I begin?
You chuckle softly, my annoyance fades,
In this clumsy affection, our love parades.

So here we lie, in our cozy test,
Each little skirmish is simply the best.
With laughter and warmth, our bond grows tight,
In this delightful struggle, all feels just right.

Tangled Hearts

In a blanket fort, we find our way,
Elbows and knees, we giggle and sway.
A battle royale for the coziest spot,
Who knew being close would be such a lot?

The dog thinks it's his, curls up with flair,
We whisper soft secrets, but he doesn't care.
Pillow fights erupt; feathers fly high,
Our hearts are all tangled, and so is the sky.

Trading warm socks to warm our toes,
Who knew cuddling could come with such woes?
Coffees spill over in fits of delight,
Fighting for space in the blanket tonight.

Huddled Hopes

When we're all wrapped up, the world fades away,
Our laughter rings bright, come what may.
A jigsaw of limbs on the oversized chair,
Crammed in together, we float like air.

TV remote wars, who'll win in the end?
As popcorn flies high, we can't make amends.
With each little bump, we giggle and clash,
Our hopes squished together like dough in a flash.

The cat jumps right in, claiming a space,
In this huddle of hopes, there's no need for grace.
Wrapped in our chaos, the night feels complete,
Together we wobble, a silly heartbeat.

The Complexity of Coziness

A cozy idea, but oh, such a feat,
With knees like carbines and toes that retreat.
Who can hold still when the snacks are around?
It's a tasty distraction, no peace can be found.

Trying to breathe in this blanket cocoon,
We laugh as we wiggle, our space is a boon.
Two heads on one pillow, that shouldn't fit right,
But we'll claim it's love as we tussle tonight.

The throw is now tangled, but spirits stay high,
Between laughter and snacks, we'll always comply.
A beautiful mess of what comfort can bring,
With chaos a-plenty, we're ready to sing.

Close Quarters

Sardines in blankets, who would have guessed?
We shuffled and laughed, I thought I'd take rest.
Tiny toes tickling, nice warmth all around,
But why does my shoulder feel quite like a mound?

A phone starts to buzz, and here comes the show,
A dance of mishaps in our tiny tableau.
With each little wriggle, we stumble like fools,
In this circus of cuddles, oh how it drools!

The dog sneezes loudly, the cat makes a fuss,
In close, crazy quarters, we tumble and cuss.
Yet despite the chaos, our hearts sing a song,
In huddled adventures, this is where we belong.

Wild Hearts

With wild little giggles in our close little nest,
We fight for the blanket, the comfort is best.
A tumble and turn, who'll win the big prize?
With tickles and snickers, we give little sighs.

The couch may be tiny, but dreams grow so wide,
Each laugh is a treasure, we share with great pride.
The wildest of hearts, we revel and fawn,
In the messy remnants of a night that's well-spawned.

Sharing the warmth, our antics declared,
In this fray of joy, we never are scared.
With snorts and with snickers, we wiggle with flair,
All wrapped in the wildness that we choose to share.

Milton Keynes UK
Ingram Content Group UK Ltd.
UKHW022116251124
451529UK00012B/555

9 789916 942093